Somewhere near you stands a
just like the wondrous 1

Mr Leafy and Friends

Written by
Rebecca Claire

Illustrated by
Sarah-Leigh Wills

Mr Leafy is a beautiful tree, a wondrous sight for all to see; he stands tall, branches swaying high in the sky, witnessing things not always noticed by you and I.

Can you guess what he can see as he stands
viewing the world majestically?

He sees fluffy-tailed rabbits hopping by,
and beautiful brown hares leaping high.

Mr Leafy sees lots of children playing on the swings
and hears adults talking about all sorts of things!

He experiences hugs from many boys and girls, parents and grandparents, aunts and uncles as well.

Mr Leafy observes birds flying in the sky and he feels
them nestle into their nests when the evening draws nigh.

He feels his leaves rustle as the squirrels scurry through; across his strong, woody branches and down his trunk, too.

Mr Leafy hears cars passing by, and emergency vehicles race, with their sirens on high.

He gazes at the aeroplanes soaring in the sky, and enjoys watching hot air balloons as they float peacefully by.

He watches the stream meander, ducks dipping and diving in and out, proud swans passing gracefully as they parade their cygnets about.

Mr Leafy can view horses and ponies grazing and frolicking in the fields. He watches farmers tending to their animals, and tractors being driven across grassy hills.

Mr Leafy observes crickets and grasshoppers chirp noisily as they jump up and down.

He feels worms, moles and insects tickle
his roots as they work hard underground.

He hears the bees buzzing as they go about their day,
pollinating the plants and flowers, making honey in their
own special way.

He finds himself home to a spider or two; they spin their
delicate webs which glisten gloriously in the morning dew.

There are so many things that surround and help
Mr Leafy - the animals, the insects, the weather,
you and me.

Mr Leafy witnesses the seasons come and go
- spring,

summer,

autumn,

winter,

the sun, the rain, the wind and the snow.

As the nights draw near and the evenings get dark, the sights Mr Leafy sees touch his heart. The owls go hoot and search for their food, whilst the badgers and foxes are out playing too.

The people all go home to their beds
and rest their tired and weary heads.

The adults read stories to children just like you, and there are plenty of wondrous sights for Mr Leafy to view.

Mr Leafy never sleeps; he sees many sights as he stands majestically all day and night.

If he could talk, he would tell you a tale or two. Look after Mr Leafy and his friends and they will help look after you.

Facts about Mr Leafy

Mr Leafy and his friends provide oxygen to help you to breathe; they also absorb carbon dioxide, and filter pollutants through their leaves. They need the sun and the rain to keep them well fed, and space to grow to provide their inhabitants with a bed.

They will provide you with shelter or an activity or two, maybe for art work; or to play 'peekaboo!'.

Mr Leafy and his friends communicate to each other via their roots, see if you can hear what they are saying when you next put on your walking boots.

Outdoor activities involving Mr Leafy and friends

Tree rubbings

Pooh sticks

Running through the fallen autumn leaves

Leaf rubbings

Leaf pictures

Twig rafts

Bug hunting

Make fairy wands or catapults

Den building

Tree hugging.

Dedicated to
"Adam, Ryan and Edward"

Mr Leafy and Friends

Copyright © 2019 Rebecca Claire.

LITTLE BAY BOOKS

Published by Little Bay books.
rebeccaclairestories.com

ISBN: 978-1-9160001-0-0

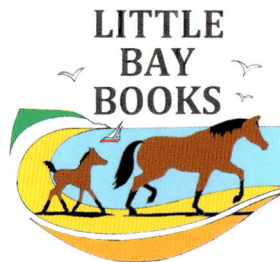

Illustration and design by Sarah-Leigh Wills.
www.happydesigner.co.uk